The
SECRET GARDEN
DAYBOOK

illustrated by

GRAHAM RUST

JANUARY

1	
2	
3	
4	

5

6

7

8

9

10 THURSDAY

13

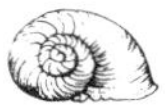

JANUARY

11	TO NYC
12	
13	HOME

*The carriage lamps shed
a yellow light on a
rough-looking road
which seemed to be cut
through bushes and low-
growing things which
ended in the great
expanse of dark
apparently spread out
before and around them.
A wind was rising and
making a singular, wild
low, rushing sound.*

JANUARY

14

15 UP-ON-THE-ROOF NOON
[5]

16 LIBRARY 4:30

17

18 Dr. LEHMAN 9:30
JENNIFER TO USSR
DINNER IN LENOX

19 DINNER HERE: DOUCLASES, MADISONS B.KUR.

JANUARY

20

21

22 TRUSTEES LIBE — 4PM.

2

23

24 TO NEW YORK

25

26	
27	JENNIFER HOME
28	ANNUAL MEETING - 4-6 PM.
29	DR. HAJJAR 10:00
30	
31	

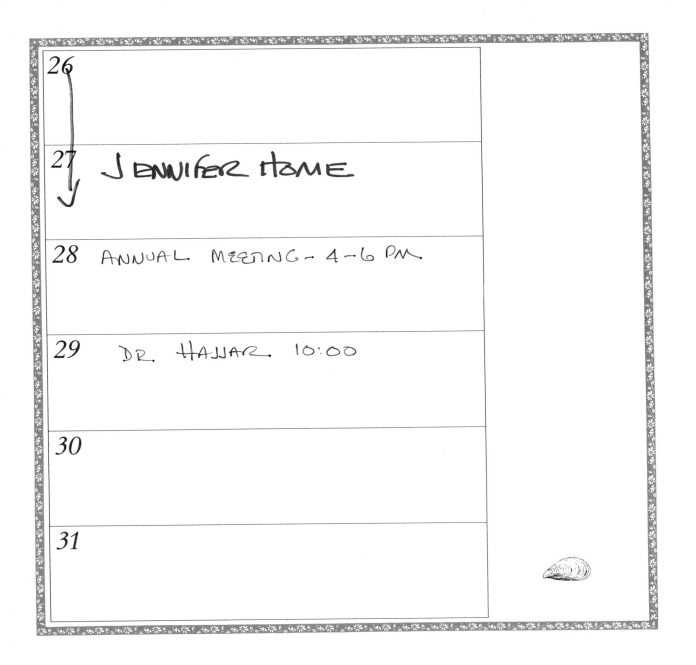

FEBRUARY

1	
2	
3	WCC BOARD
4	

5   LIBRARY TRUSTEES

6

She had just paused and was looking up at a long spray of ivy swinging in the wind, when she saw a gleam of scarlet and heard a brilliant chirp.

FEBRUARY

7

8

9

10

11

There was a laurel-hedged walk which curved round the secret garden and ended at a gate which opened into a wood in the park. She thought she would skip round this walk and look into the wood and see if there were any rabbits hopping about.

12

13

14

15

FEBRUARY

16

17

18

19

20

21

22

23

. . . it was an old key which looked as if it had been buried a long time. Mistress Mary stood up and looked at it with an almost frightened face as it hung from her finger. 'Perhaps it has been buried for ten years,' she said in a whisper. 'Perhaps it is the key to the garden!'

FEBRUARY

24

25

26

27

28

29

MARCH

1

2

3

4

5

6

7

MARCH

She was standing inside
the secret garden . . . It
was the sweetest, most
mysterious-looking place
anyone could imagine.
The high walls which
shut it in were covered
with the leafless stems of
climbing roses, which
were so thick that they
were matted together.

MARCH

8

9

10

11

12

13

14

15

16

17

18

19 TUESDAY   8 PM
JOHN IRVING AT   NYWI

MARCH

20

21

22

23

24

25

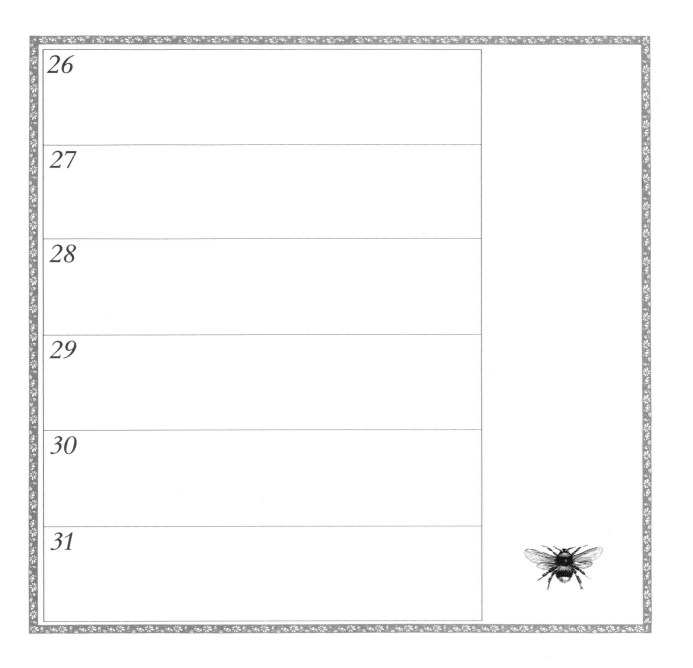

26

27

28

29

30

31

APRIL

| 1 |
| 2 |
| 3 |
| 4 |

5

6

7

8

9

10

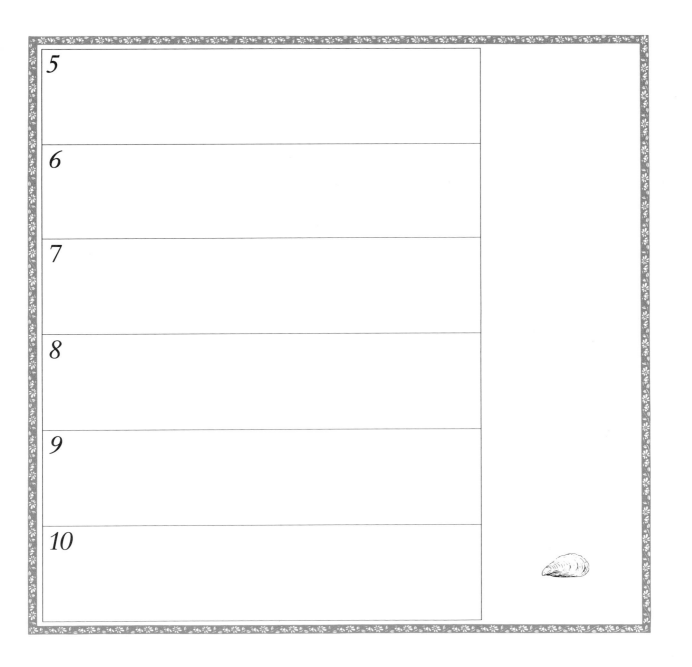

11

12

13

14

15

16

17

18

19

20

APRIL

A boy was sitting under a tree, with his back against it, playing on a rough wooden pipe. He was a funny-looking boy about twelve. He looked very clean and his nose turned up and his cheeks were as red as poppies, and never had Mistress Mary seen such round and such blue eyes in any boy's face.

21

22

23

24

APRIL

25

26

27

28

29

30

When she stepped to the wall and lifted the hanging ivy he started. There was a door and Mary pushed it slowly open and they passed in together, and then Mary stood and waved her hand round defiantly. 'It's this,' she said. 'It's a secret garden, and I'm the only one in the world who wants it to be alive.'

MAY

1

2

3

4

5

6

7

8

9

10

11

12

13

14

15

*They went from bush to
bush and from tree to tree.
He was very strong and
clever with his knife and
knew how to cut the dry
and dead wood away, and
could tell when an un-
promising bough or twig
had still green life in it.*

16

MAY

17

18

19

20

21

22

23

24

25

. . . and under the apple-
tree was lying a little
reddish animal with a
bushy tail, and both of
them were watching the
stooping body and rust-
red head of Dickon, who
was kneeling on the grass
working hard. 'This is
th' little fox cub,' he said,
rubbing the little reddish
animal's head. 'It's
named Captain.'

MAY

26

27

28

29

30

31

The moor was hidden in mist when the morning came, and the rain had not stopped pouring down. There could be no going out of doors.

JUNE

1

2

3

4

5

6

7

8

9

10

JUNE

11

12

13

14

15

16

Swiftly something flew across the wall and darted through the trees to a close-grown corner, a little flare of red-breasted bird with something hanging from its beak . . . 'It's part o' th' springtime, this nest-buildin' is,' he said. 'I warrant it's been goin' on in th' same way every year since th' world was begun.'

JUNE

17

18

19

20

21

22

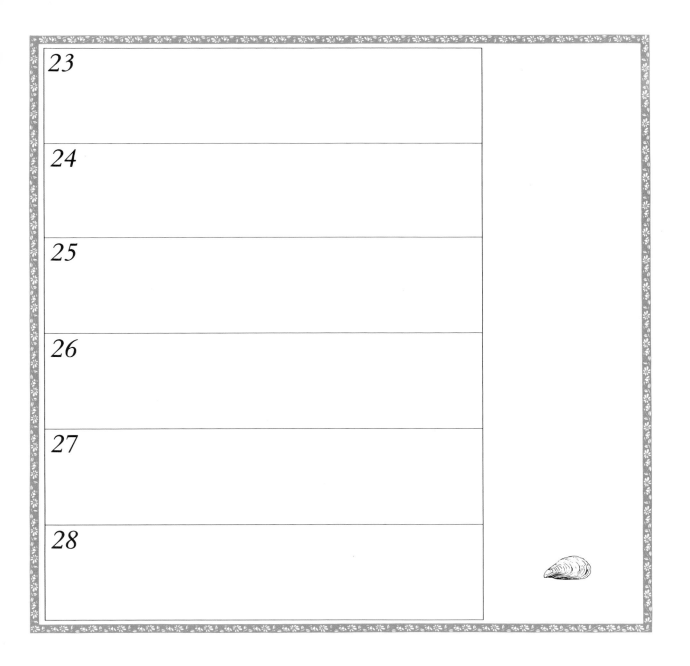

23

24

25

26

27

28

JUNE

29

30

JULY

1	
2	
3	
4	

JULY

5

6

7

8

9

10

11

12

13

14

15

16

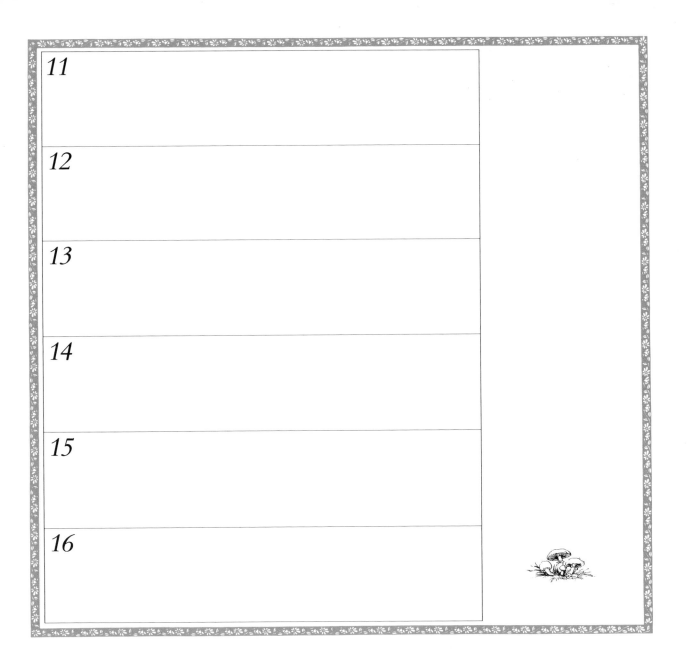

JULY

17

18

19

20

21

22

*Sometimes the rook
flapped his black wings
and soared away over the
tree-tops in the park.
Each time he came back
and perched near Dickon
and cawed several times
as if he were relating his
adventures, and Dickon
talked to him just as he
had talked to the robin.
Once when Dickon was
so busy that he did not
answer him at first, Soot
flew on to his shoulder
and gently tweaked his
ear with his large beak.*

JULY

23

24

25

26

27

28

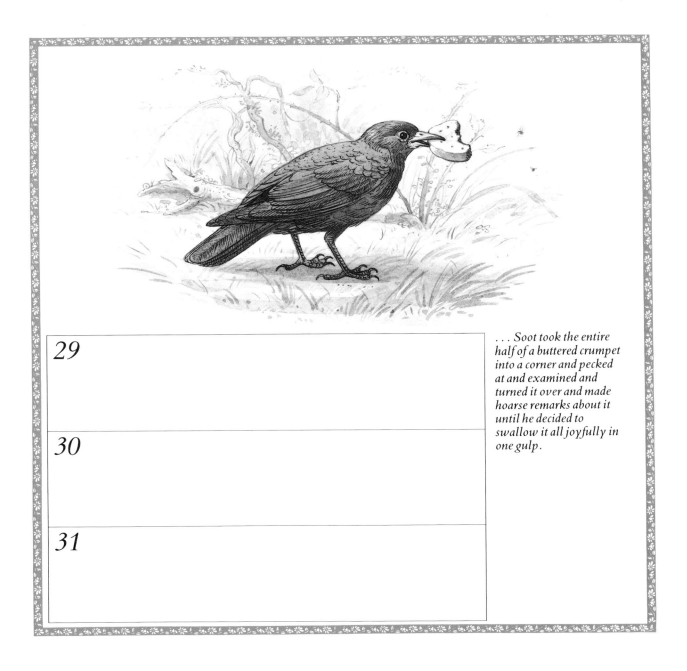

29

30

31

. . . Soot took the entire half of a buttered crumpet into a corner and pecked at and examined and turned it over and made hoarse remarks about it until he decided to swallow it all joyfully in one gulp.

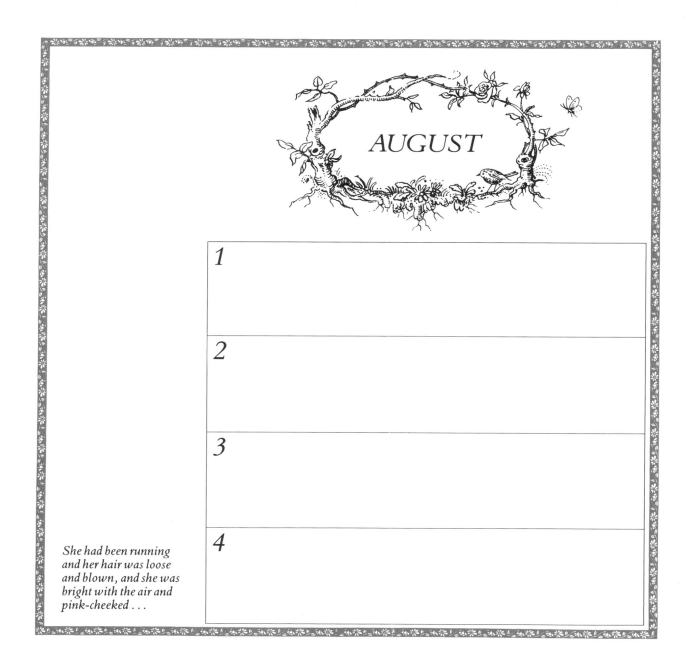

AUGUST

1

2

3

4

*She had been running
and her hair was loose
and blown, and she was
bright with the air and
pink-cheeked . . .*

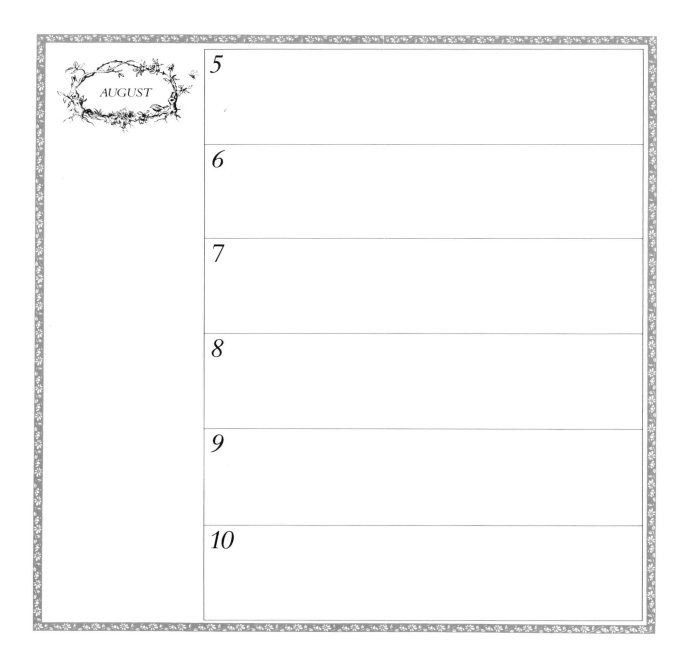

AUGUST

5

6

7

8

9

10

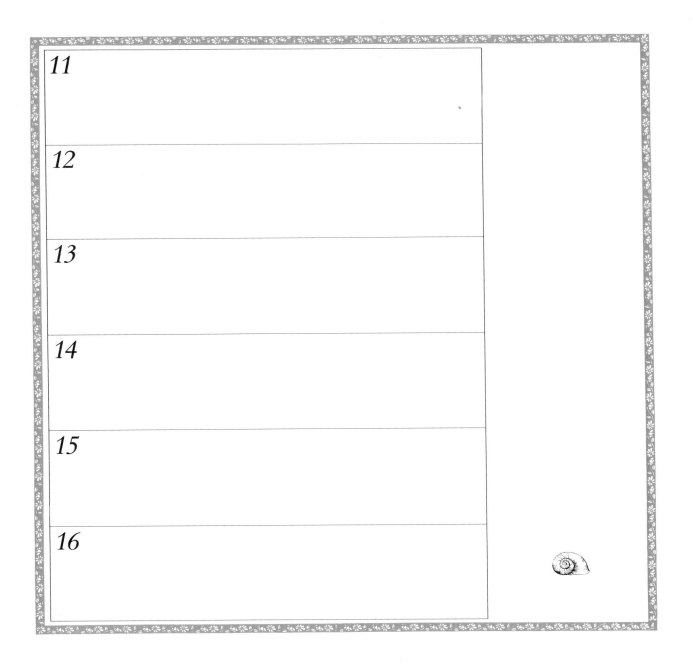

11

12

13

14

15

16

AUGUST

17

18

19

20

And this, if you please, this is what Ben Weatherstaff beheld and which made his jaw drop. A wheeled-chair with luxurious cushions and robes which came towards him looking rather like some sort of state coach because a young rajah leaned back in it with royal command in his great, black-rimmed eyes and a thin white hand extended haughtily towards him.

21

22

AUGUST

23

24

25

26

27

28

29
30
31

Ben Weatherstaff walked behind, and the 'creatures' trailed after them . . . keeping close to Dickon, the white rabbit hopping along or stopping to nibble . . .

SEPTEMBER

1

2

3

4

Dickon held his rabbit in his arm, and perhaps he made some charmer's signal no one heard, for when he sat down, cross-legged like the rest, the crow, the fox, the squirrels, and the lamb drew near and made part of the circle, settling each into a place of rest as if of their own desire.

SEPTEMBER

5

6

7

8

9

10

11

12

13

14

15

16

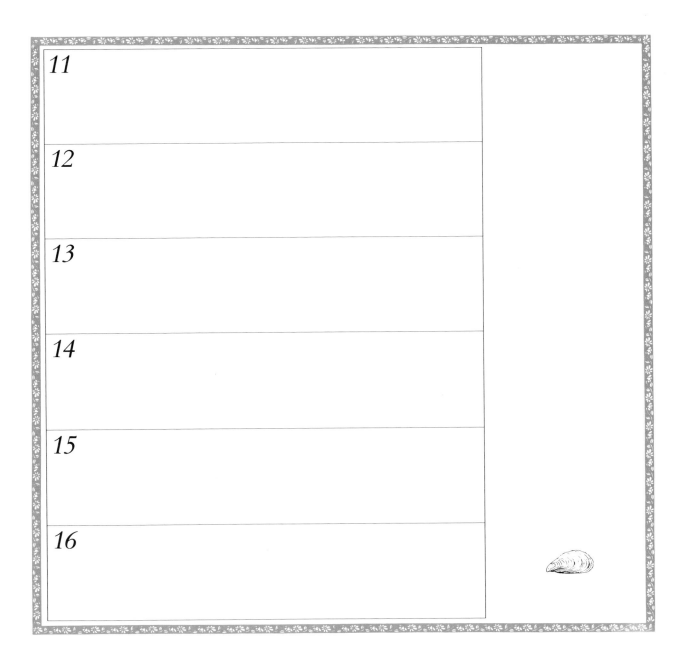

17

18

19

20

21

22

23

24

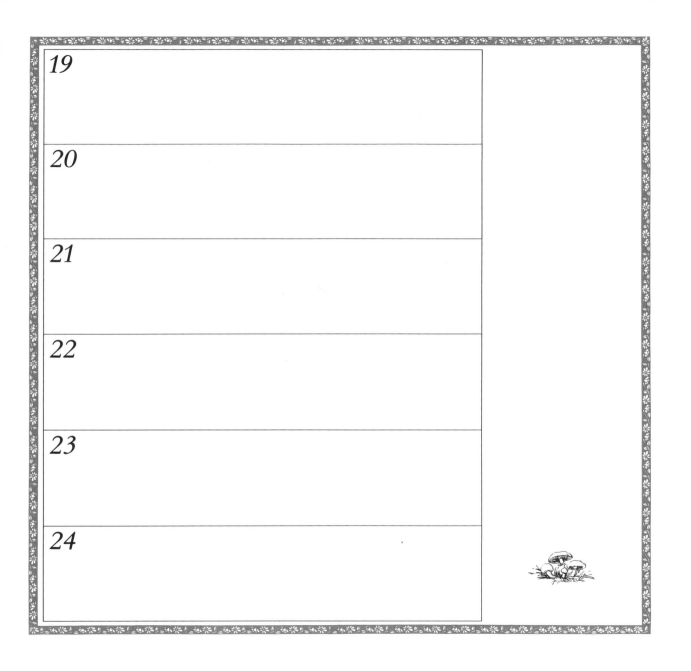

25

26

27

28

29

30

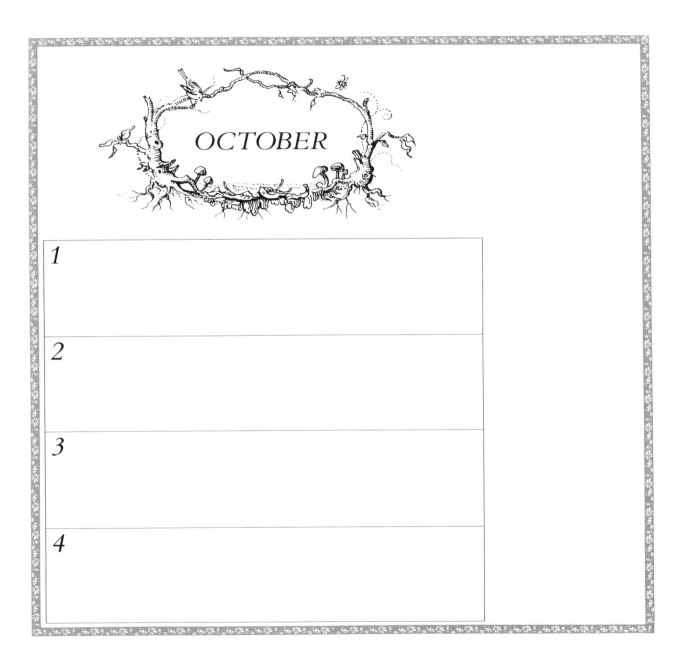

OCTOBER

1

2

3

4

OCTOBER

5

6

7

8

9

10

Dickon made the stimulating discovery that in the wood in the park outside the garden where Mary had first found him piping to the wild creatures, there was a deep little hollow where you could build a sort of tiny oven with stones and roast potatoes and eggs...

OCTOBER

11

12

13

14

15

16

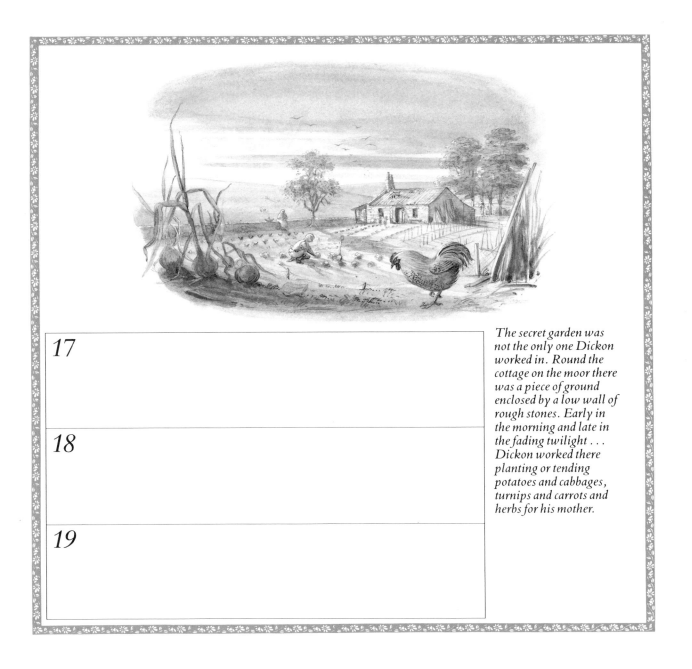

17

18

19

The secret garden was not the only one Dickon worked in. Round the cottage on the moor there was a piece of ground enclosed by a low wall of rough stones. Early in the morning and late in the fading twilight . . . Dickon worked there planting or tending potatoes and cabbages, turnips and carrots and herbs for his mother.

OCTOBER

20

21

22

23

24

25

26

27

28

29

30

31

NOVEMBER

1

2

3

4

5

6

7

8

9

10

NOVEMBER

11

12

13

14

15

16

17

18

19

20

21

22

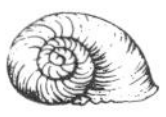

NOVEMBER

23

24

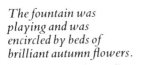

*The fountain was
playing and was
encircled by beds of
brilliant autumn flowers.*

NOVEMBER

25

26

27

28

29

30

DECEMBER

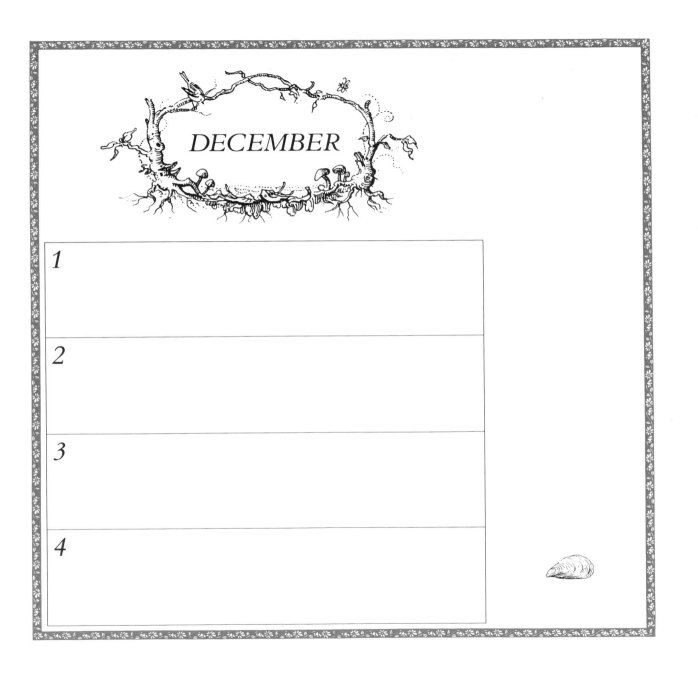

1
2
3
4

DECEMBER

5

6

7

8

9

10

11

12

13

14

15

16

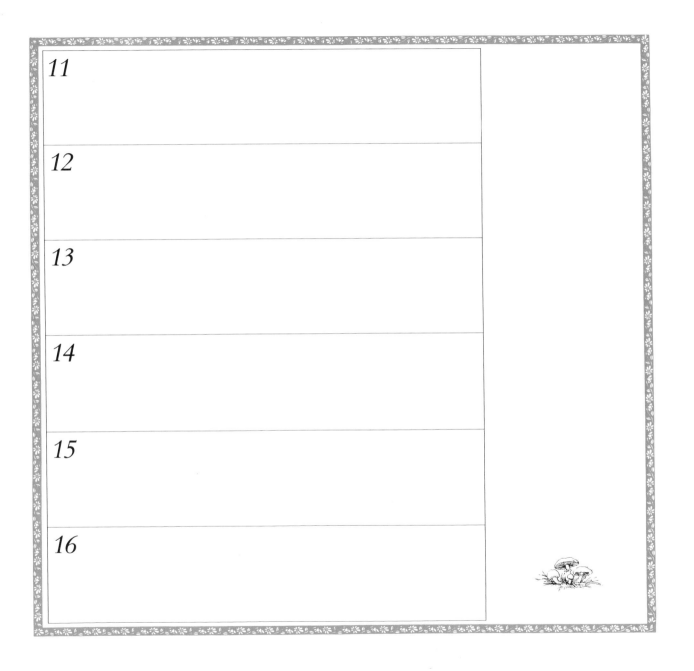

17

18

19

DECEMBER

The place was a wilderness of autumn gold and purple and violet and flaming scarlet.

DECEMBER

20

21

22

23

24

25

26

27

28

29

30

31

Conceived and produced by
Breslich & Foss
Golden House
28–31 Great Pulteney Street
London W1R 3DD

Designed by Roger Daniels

First published in the United States
by David R. Godine Publisher Inc.
Horticultural Hall
300 Massachusetts Avenue
Boston, Massachusetts 02115

ISBN 0-87923-747-3